SAN ANTONIO SPURS

NBA CHAMPIONS

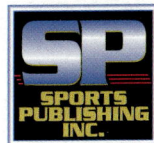

C0-BUU-159

Northwest Vista College
Learning Resource Center
3535 North Ellison Drive
San Antonio, Texas 78251

NORTHWEST VISTA COLLEGE

San Antonio Spurs nb

34009000124470

Published by Sports Publishing Inc.
www.SportsPublishingInc.com

SAN ANTONIO SPURS: NBA CHAMPIONS

SP
SPORTS
PUBLISHING
INC.

JOANNA L. WRIGHT, Coordinating Editor

SUSAN M. MCKINNEY, Production Director
TERRY N. HAYDEN, Interior Design
TERRY N. HAYDEN, Dustjacket Design

AP/WIDE WORLD PHOTOS, Front and back cover photos and all interior photos

Copyright © 1999 Sports Publishing Inc. All rights reserved.

ISBN 1-58261-192-0

Published by Sports Publishing Inc.
www.SportsPublishingInc.com

Printed in the United States

DAVID ROBINSON AND TIM DUNCAN
EXCHANGE A HIGH FIVE DURING THE FIRST
HALF OF GAME 5 AGAINST THE KNICKS.

SPURS (FROM LEFT) TIM DUNCAN, ANTONIO DANIELS, DAVID ROBINSON, GERARD KING, SEAN ELLIOTT, AVERY JOHNSON AND JEROME KERSEY celebrate on the floor of MADISON SQUARE GARDEN after winning THE TEAM'S FIRST NBA TITLE.

DAVID ROBINSON HUGS HIS FATHER, AMBROSE, WHILE
HOLDING HIS SON, DAVID JR., AFTER WINNING THE NBA
CHAMPIONSHIP.

GREGG POPOVICH HUGS FINALS MVP TIM DUNCAN
AFTER THE SPURS CLINCH THE NBA TITLE.

MARIO ELIE CELEBRATES AFTER THE SPURS BEAT THE
KNICKS, 78-77, TO CLAIM THEIR FIRST NBA CHAMPIONSHIP.

AVERY
JOHNSON,
DAVID
ROBINSON,
ANTONIO
DANIELS AND
MARIO ELIE
(FROM BOT-
TOM) ARE
GREETED BY
FANS AS THEY
RETURN TO
SAN ANTONIO.

Tim Duncan (left) and Antonio Daniels cheer
the crowd during the victory parade along the
Riverwalk.

SPURS CAPTAINS DAVID ROBINSON AND
AVERY JOHNSON REACT TO THE CROWD DUR-
ING THE PARADE.

MARIO ELIE SHOOTS OVER KURT THOMAS AND ALLAN
HOUSTON OF THE KNICKS IN GAME 2 OF THE NBA FINALS.

ELIE BRINGS SHOOTING, LEADERSHIP, PASSION TO SPURS

BY KELLEY SHANNON   APRIL 15, 1999

SAN ANTONIO (AP)—With his hard-driving spirit and ferocious bark, Mario Elie takes pride in his reputation as a junkyard dog.

"I'm a pit bull," Elie said with a devilish grin. "I'm going to be on guys. I'm going to be hard on myself. I'm going to go out there, play hard.

"I'm going to elbow. I'm going to get into scuffles. I'm going to talk trash with the bench. I'm going to do everything to get my team going."

That's what the San Antonio Spurs like about their new starting guard. It doesn't hurt that Elie also has a mean 3-pointer and knows what it takes to win a championship.

Elie played in Houston when the Rockets won NBA titles in 1994 and 1995 and remained there through last year. As a free agent, Elie signed with the Spurs before the start of this lockout-shortened season.

Equipped with 7-footers David Robinson and Tim Duncan and assorted experienced role players, San Antonio didn't lack talent. But the Spurs have been branded as a squad lacking emotion, raising questions about whether the team can win a title.

This is Robinson's 10th year in the league. In his first nine seasons, the Spurs were ousted from the playoffs in the first round three times and made it past the second round only once—in 1995, when they lost to the Rockets.

On several occasions, Robinson's postseason performance has been disappointing, prompting some to call him soft. Elie is trying to change all that as quickly as he can.

"I don't have anything personal against those guys, but they know I want to win," Elie said. "So when David is not aggressive, Tim is not aggressive, I'll grab them by the jersey and say, 'You guys got to get tougher.' The guys are like, 'All right, Mario.'"

Elie describes Robinson as a corporate All-Star because he "comes to work with his suit on, goes out there, does his job," while showing little emotion.

"I've been working with him. He's been getting a little fiery, " Elie said. "He got a technical foul. ... He clenched his fist a couple of times. That's progress."

Elie's determined attitude and passion for winning were what Spurs coach Gregg Popovich sought.

"Mario has been huge for us," Popovich said. "He does all the blue-collar things. He's got toughness, he has leadership skills. He's just sort of a junkyard dog. The guy just will do whatever it takes to win."

Elie began the season coming off the bench for the Spurs but has replaced Jaren Jackson in the starting lineup. Elie has been averaging more than 10 points per game.

Elie was drafted and waived by Milwaukee in 1985. He played in Portugal, Argentina and Ireland, and in the CBA, USBL and WBL before NBA teams started hiring him in 1990.

His playoff experience with Houston, Portland and Golden State taught him about winning and losing in the postseason. Elie has always been vocal, but his two championships make fellow players pay particular attention when he speaks now.

"Toughness, toughness, toughness," Spurs point guard Avery Johnson says, describing Elie. "When he walks on the court, he's well respected."

At the same time the Spurs added Elie, they traded with Chicago for Steve Kerr and signed free agent Jerome Kersey—all players with playoff resumes.

"It's just the years of being in the wars," Elie said. "We've been to the promised land. We know what it takes to get there. It's not just talent, but you need a little edge, a little fire."

The pressure of a playoff-elimination game is enormous, he said. You can't sleep the night before. The world is watching. And if you lose, your friends call and say you choked.

"There's a lot that goes into a situation like that. The bottom line is wins and losses."

Winning a title is a feeling like no other, Elie added.

"It's just a feeling of being the best team on Earth, man. It's just the best feeling. It's what you play for," he said.

Elie, 35, figures he has only a couple of years left in the league, and he wants another championship. He believes a title is within reach for San Antonio.

"They're starting to think championship, finally, instead of just going to the third round in the play-offs," he said. "You've got to think of winning it all."

MARIO ELIE TALKS WITH THE MEDIA AFTER PRACTICE IN SAN ANTONIO.

PASSION

MARIO ELIE, DAVID ROBINSON

Over the years, the Spurs have acquired a reputation as a team that lacks emotion. The arrival of Mario Elie has changed all that. Elie's passion has been getting his team fired up, and his emotion while playing has begun rubbing off on his quieter teammates. Above, Elie (left) cheers from the bench during a game against Detroit. David Robinson (right), perhaps the most-criticized for his perceived lack of emotion, cheers as his team takes the lead late in Game 2 of the Western Conference Finals against Portland.

MALIK ROSE BATTLES CHRIS MILLS OF THE GOLDEN STATE WAR-
RIORS FOR A LOOSE BALL.

SPURS RESERVES READY AFTER SWEEP OF LAKERS

BY KELLEY SHANNON   MAY 25, 1999

SAN ANTONIO (AP)—Jaren Jackson, Malik Rose and their buddies on the Spurs bench have played a quiet but important role in San Antonio's success all season.

In the playoffs, the reserves are shining almost as brightly as the Spurs' big stars.

"We're all coming off the bench trying to help this team get as many wins as possible," Rose said. "We really take pride in coming in and changing the flow of the game."

As the Spurs waited Tuesday to find out whether they'll face Portland or Utah in the Western Conference finals, several Spurs reserves took part in an optional workout at the Alamodome.

"Just keep a sweat going every day, try to stay loose and fit and be ready to focus on the next game, whenever it comes," said Jackson, who scored a career playoff-high 22 points on Saturday in the Spurs' Game 3 victory over the Lakers.

Jackson followed with 20 points on Sunday as the Spurs swept the best-of-7 series 4-0.

Jackson, a guard who began the season as a starter, was replaced in that role by Mario Elie several games into the season. Jackson's performance as a reserve blossomed as the playoffs arrived.

Though he'd been a little stiff early in the Lakers series, Jackson said he got some rest and felt good entering the final two games.

"I just let my game come to me. I was a little bit more aggressive, " he said. "I just wanted to make sure I did my share coming off the bench."

Rose was one of several San Antonio players assigned to guard Shaquille O'Neal during the series. Rose also scored 13 points and had five rebounds in Game 2 and scored eight points in Game 4.

"You guys are just noticing it," Rose told reporters. "But for the entire season the bench has been playing well."

On any given night, Rose said, he, Jackson, Jerome Kersey or another reserve comes through with a strong game.

Spurs center David Robinson has said that with some teams, bench players can only be expected to hold their own until the starters return. With the San Antonio reserves on the court, a run can get going and the defensive intensity remains high.

In the first game of the Lakers series, the San Antonio reserves outscored the Los Angeles reserves 17-2. Will Perdue came off the bench to grab nine rebounds, more than any other Spurs player.

In Game 3, Spurs reserves outrebounded Lakers reserves 19-8.

In Sunday's fourth game, Kersey scored five points and Jackson hit a 3-pointer in a 13-0 Spurs run to start the final quarter. Jackson hit six 3-pointers in the game, and Kersey scored all nine of his points in the fourth period.

Rose has a nickname for the bench guys.

"We're all collectively the 'bum rush,'" he said. "There's no one bigger than the other."

Jackson plans to continue trying to improve the reputation of the Spurs' guards, both starters and reserves.

"It just so happens that we all collectively have done a pretty good job," he said. "We just do what it takes to help the team win."

JAREN JACKSON AND UTAH'S JOHN HORNACEK VIE FOR THE BALL DURING A GAME IN SAN ANTONIO.

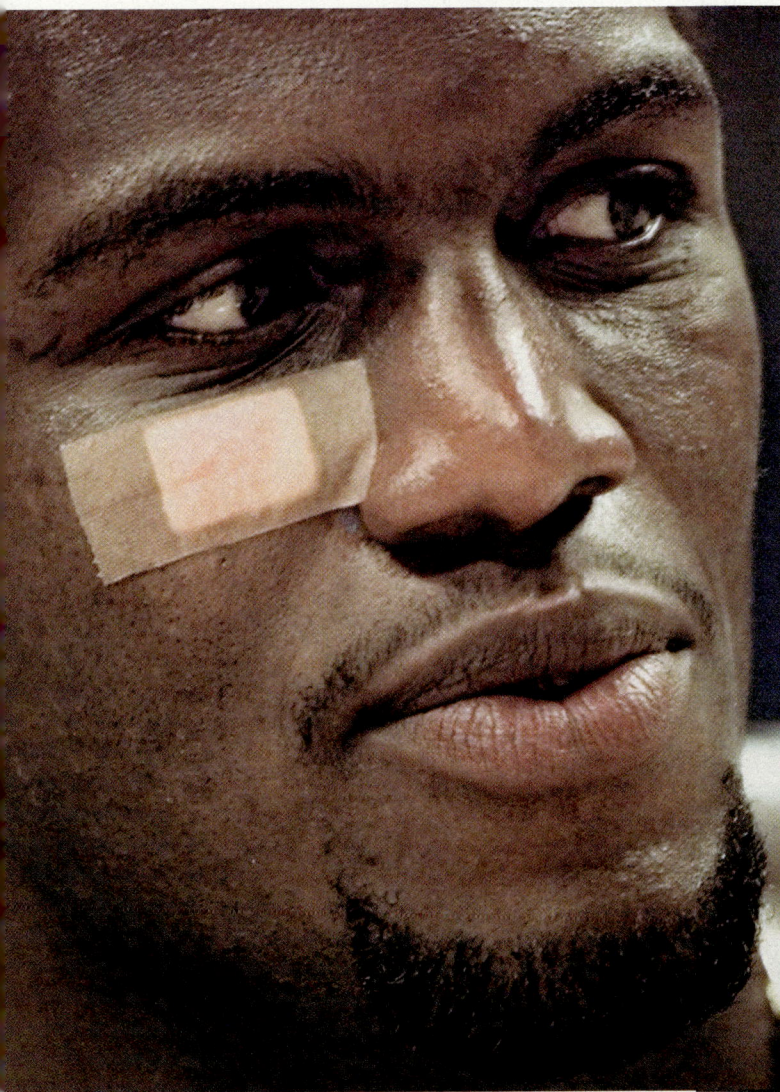

TEAMWORK

Throughout the season, the Spurs' bench was an integral part of their success. Even though they weren't starting, the reserves took pride in being able to maintain intensity, change the flow of a game and contribute to their team's success—the essence of teamwork. The bench's contributions continued through the playoffs, with various players providing whatever the Spurs happened to need at the time. Reserve forward Malik Rose (above) sports a bandage during practice after receiving a cut under the eye in Game 1 of the NBA Finals. At right, Will Perdue congratulates Tim Duncan in the closing seconds of a victory over the Lakers.

SEAN ELLIOTT struggles to keep his balANCE WHILE TRYING TO PASS THE BALL PAST
A DEFENDER.

ELLIOTT BASKS IN CELEBRITY AFTER "THE SHOT"

BY BOB BAUM   JUNE 2, 1999

PORTLAND, Oregon (AP)—It's already known in San Antonio as "The Shot."

Sean Elliott's off-balance, on his tip-toes, almost out-of-bounds 3-pointer that beat Portland in Game 2 of the Western Conference finals is almost certainly the biggest basket in the franchise's history and ranks with some of the toughest game-winning shots in NBA playoff history.

"I'm just grateful that the ball went in," Elliott said when he showed up for the Spurs' optional workout on Tuesday in San Antonio. "If people want to remember me for that, so be it."

He said maybe the Spurs' devoutly Christian players—David Robinson and Avery Johnson—deserve credit for the two close homecourt victories that put the Spurs up 2-0 in the best-of-seven series.

"I think we have to thank somebody," Elliott said. "We have to thank David and Avery for praying so much. Somebody answered our prayers."

Elliott said he's watched the replay of his game winner "a couple of dozen times." Meanwhile, the phone at his house has been ringing constantly.

"I got a million calls," he said. "I've got everybody calling me. I had a couple of old coaches calling me, practically everybody."

Johnson said by making six of seven 3-pointers in Game 2, Elliott could change the Blazers' defensive strategy, which mostly has been to collapse on Tim Duncan and David Robinson.

"I think they're going to pay a little more attention to Sean," Johnson said. "Maybe that may free up some more penetration from our perimeter guys, especially Mario and myself."

The Spurs planned to practice in San Antonio today before traveling to Portland, where the series doesn't resume until Friday.

The Blazers, who took Tuesday off, can use every minute of the long layoff to repair their psyche.

"I think it is the toughest loss that we've had all season," Damon Stoudamire said. "But the good thing about this is ... we've got three days to regroup, and then they're going to come into a hostile environment in Portland."

The Blazers led by as many as 18 points and didn't trail in the game until Elliott's game-winner with nine seconds to play.

"It took incredible shots to beat us," Portland coach Mike Dunleavy said. "I'd give (Elliott) 100 bucks to see him make that shot again. It was one of those shots you dream about making ... I told the guys they have nothing to hang their heads about. It's getting harder and harder for this team to beat us."

San Antonio coach Gregg Popovich said the momentum of the miracle comeback probably won't last until the weekend.

"If we were coming back and playing tomorrow, it would be huge, " he said. "But Friday is like 2 1/2 weeks from now. Nobody will even be able to remember this game."

The Spurs' eight-game playoff winning streak will be tested in the noisy Rose Garden, where the Blazers lost just three times during the regular season and are 5-0 in the playoffs.

Still, Portland must win four out of five, including at least once in the Alamodome, to advance to the finals.

"I don't see why we can't," Greg Anthony said. "We're a real confident basketball team. We're a real talented basketball team."

SEAN ELLIOTT LEAVES THE COURT
IN THE ALAMODOME AFTER HIS
GAME-WINNING SHOT.

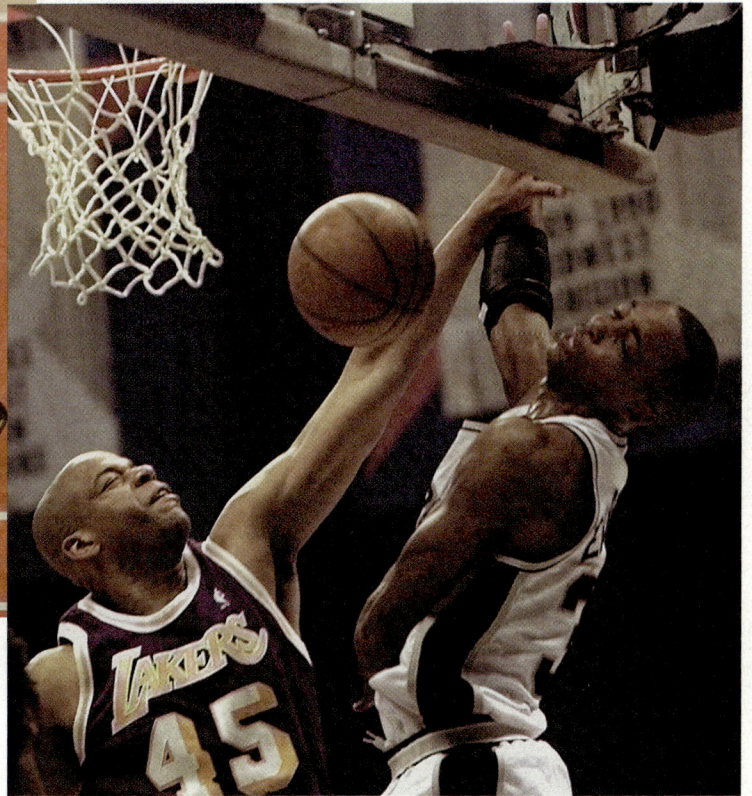

SACRIFICE

The members of a successful team make sacrifices. They sacrifice their egos. They sacrifice their time. They sacrifice their energy. When it's necessary, they even "sacrifice their bodies." Above left, David Robinson draws the offensive foul from Allan Houston during Game 4 of the NBA Finals against the Knicks. Above right, Sean Elliott risks the foul while going up against Sean Rooks of the Los Angeles Lakers.

DAVID ROBINSON REACTS TO SEAN ELLIOTT'S "SHOT" IN THE FINAL SECONDS OF GAME 2 OF THE WESTERN CONFERENCE FINALS AGAINST PORTLAND.

SPURS WIN WESTERN CONFERENCE TITLE

BY BOB BAUM   JUNE 7, 1999

PORTLAND, Oregon (AP)—In the moments after the San Antonio Spurs clinched their first trip to the NBA Finals in the 23 years since the franchise joined the league, David Robinson spoke to his teammates behind a closed locker room door.

He wanted to thank them and tell them how much they meant to him. After 10 years of criticism that he's too soft or couldn't win the big one, The Admiral was bringing the fleet home in triumph.

"You should have heard him," Tim Duncan said. "It means so much to him. He's worked so many years and this is the first time he's gotten there. What he said is that this is the best that he's felt with a team, looking at all the people on the floor that he knows he can count on."

Avery Johnson knew how much the sweep of Portland in the Western Conference finals, completed with a masterful 94-80 victory on Sunday, meant to Robinson. Johnson remembered 1995, when Robinson was the league's MVP but the Spurs were knocked off by Houston in the conference finals.

"Like I always tell you all, I would love to win a championship," Johnson said. "I really would love to win it. That's what I am here for. But I want to see David win it more than myself. He's a terrific man, and I've been with him for years."

Robinson had 20 points and 10 rebounds and again was a force on defense, stifling repeated attempts by Portland to score inside.

"It's been 10 long years, but it's just what I imagined it would be like," Robinson said. "You work so hard. It feels really good to finally get there."

The Spurs won their 10th straight postseason game, one short of the league record. Since a shaky 6-8 start, San Antonio is 42-6, a record that even Michael Jordan and the Chicago Bulls would have admired.

"It feels unbelievable," Sean Elliott said. "We're just on a huge high right now, but at the same time we realize that we have a lot more work to do."

First, though, comes a lot more waiting. The Spurs must return to San Antonio to await the outcome of the Eastern Conference finals, where New York has a 2-1 lead on Indiana. The NBA Finals won't start until next Sunday, at the earliest. Robinson won't mind the wait.

"We have, how should I put it, a lot of seasoned players on this team," he said. "We can use the rest."

It was that seasoning that made a big difference against the young, emotional Blazers. San Antonio was unflappable, even when the Blazers rallied to briefly take the lead in the third quarter.

**AVERY JOHNSON SMILES FROM THE BENCH AS THE SPURS DE-
FEAT THE TRAIL BLAZERS IN GAME 3 OF THE WESTERN
CONFRENCE FINALS.**

Duncan had two three-point plays, a spectacular slam dunk and a series of big defensive plays to help the Spurs pull away. The Blazers came away impressed.

"I don't know if they'll sweep, but I predict they'll win it all," Brian Grant said. "And I'm not saying that just because they beat us. They're tough. They've set themselves up to be champions."

San Antonio put away the biggest victory ever with a 17-4 run in the fourth quarter. Duncan and Elliott each scored five points and Johnson had four in the decisive surge. The first of Jaren Jackson's three 3-pointers in the fourth quarter put the Spurs up 81-67 with 7:09 to play.

Duncan, who had just five points in Game 3, had 18 points and eight rebounds in Game 4. Elliott scored 16. Johnson, the point guard Damon Stoudamire said would never lead a team to a championship, had 15 points and six assists.

Stoudamire talked with Johnson for a moment just as the game ended.

"I told him he's proving a lot of people wrong," Stoudamire said.

San Antonio is 11-1 in the playoffs, 6-0 on the road. After winning the first-round series with Minnesota 3-1, the Spurs swept the Los Angeles Lakers and the Blazers.

The Spurs are the first of the four old ABA teams to make it to the NBA Finals. Indiana could join them if the Pacers beat the Knicks.

Never a flashy bunch, the Spurs celebrated only with hugs and high fives.

"If we win four more games, then we'll let it out and unwind a lot more," Elliott said.

CELEBRATION

DAVID ROBINSON, MARIO ELIE

After being the NBA's top draft pick in 1987, Robinson joined the Spurs in 1989 after fulfilling his Navy commitment. Throughout his 10 years in the league, Robinson has been criticized for being unable to lead his team to a championship. This year, he finally got his chance. Here, David Robinson and Mario Elie celebrate after sweeping the Portland Trail Blazers to earn the Western Conference championship and advance to the NBA Finals.

TIM DUNCAN LOOKS TO BREAK
THROUGH JIM JACKSON (LEFT)
AND GREG ANTHONY (RIGHT) DUR-
ING THE WESTERN CONFERENCE
FINALS.

WHAT MAKES THE SPURS SO GOOD?

BY BOB BAUM   JUNE 7, 1999

PORTLAND, Oregon (AP)—What makes the San Antonio Spurs so good?

Start with the obvious—Tim Duncan and David Robinson. Throw in consistent outside shooting from Avery Johnson, Sean Elliott, Jaren Jackson and Steve Kerr along with the toughness and experience of Mario Elie. Now add some serious togetherness and unselfishness.

It all adds up to a team that has won 10 playoff games in a row, sweeping the Los Angeles Lakers and Portland Trail Blazers in the process, to reach the NBA Finals for the first time in the franchise's history.

"Every man on our team is important, and I think they know it," Robinson said. "Even the guys who don't play push us in practice. I'm proud of this team. They've accepted roles. I'm proud of how far they've come. I'm having as much fun with this group as I've ever had."

The Portland Trail Blazers got a textbook lesson in what it's like to face a team with big-time talent up front and confident role players everywhere else. The defense has to double-team Duncan and Robinson, and that would leave someone else open on the outside.

"Every game they played, they seemed to get better," Portland coach Mike Dunleavy said.

The book on defending the Spurs is to concentrate on Duncan and Robinson and take the chance that the other players won't come through.

But the role players have not let the Spurs down, helping them to a 42-6 record since the team got off to a 6-8 start and fans were calling for coach Gregg Popovich to get fired.

"When we were 6-8, we had the opportunity to really turn on each other," Robinson said.

Against Portland, Elliott was a consistent threat. After an injury-plagued season last year, he became a major offensive force both with his outside shot and his ability to drive. He shot 56 percent and averaged more than 15 points a game.

"People have been double-teaming Tim and David all year long," Popovich said, "so we've had a lot of practice spreading the court with shooters. We just have to make shots or we're going to lose basketball games. When we first came out of the gate, and we were 6-8, we had no inside-outside coordination. Now we have that coordination down."

Johnson, overlooked and underappreciated around the NBA but not on his team, was 6-for-12 in Sunday's 94-80 series-clinching victory against Portland.

"WHEN YOU HAVE A LOT OF TALENT, IT'S EASY TO START POINTING FINGERS, AND WE DIDN'T DO THAT. WE DECIDED WE WOULD COME TOGETHER."

DAMON STOUDAMIRE PUSHES PAST SPURS RESERVE GUARD STEVE KERR.

Johnson's teammates know how important he is, and when the point guard slipped and bruised his knee in the second quarter Sunday, they rushed to his side.

"I was so scared," Duncan said. "He is the biggest part of our team. Knowing A.J., I knew that even if he broke his leg, he would get back up and play again. It's an incredible relief that he's OK."

Jackson, like Elie and Johnson, came up the hard way in the NBA, bouncing from team to team before finding himself the designated shooter off the bench for the Spurs. He tied a team record with six 3-pointers in the Game 3 rout of Portland, then hit three of them in the fourth quarter as San Antonio pulled away in Game 4.

Now add Kerr to the equation. After going 0-for-12 in the playoffs and struggling to find his place, Kerr settled in as backup point guard against Portland and hit a big 3-pointer in the second quarter Sunday.

"You stop one guy, and another guy gets on a roll," Duncan said. "The way we're winning shows how awesome we are."

ROLE PLAYERS

AVERY JOHNSON, JAREN JACKSON

Finally, the Spurs have all the pieces to their championship puzzle. Besides the veteran David Robinson and 1998 NBA Rookie of the Year Tim Duncan, the Spurs have several key role players on their team, including Mario Elie, Steve Kerr, Avery Johnson and Jaren Jackson. Elie and Kerr also bring NBA championship experience to the team (Elie with the Houston Rockets, Kerr with the Chicago Bulls). Avery Johnson (right) drives around Tyronn Lue of the Los Angeles Lakers, while Jaren Jackson (above) defends the Bulls' Ron Harper.

MARIO ELIE LAYS THE BALL UP WHILE BEING DEFENDED BY PORTLAND'S RASHEED WALLACE. AFTER WINNING TWO GAMES IN PORTLAND TO SWEEP THE WESTERN CONFERENCE FINALS, THE SPURS RETURNED HOME TO AWAIT THE WINNER OF THE KNICKS-PACERS SERIES IN THE EAST.

SPURS RETURN TO JUBILANT SAN ANTONIO

BY KELLEY SHANNON   **JUNE 7, 1999**

SAN ANTONIO (AP)—The San Antonio Spurs arrived home today bearing a big gift for devoted fans—their first trip to the NBA Finals.

"This is exciting. You guys have been behind us for years and years," Spurs point guard Avery Johnson told hundreds of cheering fans who greeted the team's charter plane.

"You should feel good, because you are a part of history," Johnson said.

Chanting "Go Spurs, Go!" and "Sweep, Sweep, Sweep" and carrying Spurs signs, about 3,500 people crowded around a private terminal at San Antonio International Airport to welcome the team.

Hungry for a championship after 26 years of waiting, Spurs supporters kicked into serious party mode after San Antonio won the Western Conference finals Sunday by defeating the Trail Blazers 94-80 in Portland and sweeping the series 4-0.

Cars decorated with Spurs slogans cruised the streets, horns honking. Spectators in sports bars watched the game on television, then went wild afterward. The *San Antonio Express-News* displayed a banner headline Monday declaring "SPUR-FECT."

"All I can say right now is whew!" center David Robinson said at the airport. "Our work is not finished, but I'll tell you what, we're feeling pretty good right now."

Diehard fans camped out all night at the Alamodome to buy title-round tickets, which went on sale Monday morning.

"I ran down here after the game. I was so excited," said Raul Adam, a computer consultant who was a bit breathless after purchasing the limit of six tickets each for the first and second games of the finals. The seats, in the dome's upper deck, were $25 apiece.

An exhausted Rene Riojas, a county employee, brought his 12-year-old son Rene Riojas Jr. with him to the Alamodome about 9:30 p.m. Sunday to get in line for tickets.

"I wanted my son to experience the NBA ... the NBA Finals," Riojas said. "I think it's fantastic. I think it's about time. It's the Spurs' time now, now that the Bulls are gone. I think it's good for the city."

Bruce Bennett, president of the North East School District board, and his 8-year-old son, Bradley, also went to the dome Sunday night.

"I've never camped out for anything in my life," Bennett said, with a smile and a shake of his head. "I think it's great. I've always liked the players."

Sandra Castilleja, a school employee, was not always a Spurs fan before. Like thousands of others, she has hopped on the bandwagon.

"I've lived my whole life in San Antonio and I've never been to a Spurs game," she said. "I'm a fan now."

DAVID ROBINSON AND TIM DUNCAN EXCHANGE HIGH FIVES WITH
SPURS FANS.

Spurs spirit had been taking over the city for days.

Now it's at full speed.

Spurs signs decorate a tall downtown bank tower, the windows of shops, homes and cars and even the window of a halfway house for recently released federal prisoners.

"I'm so excited for the city of San Antonio," Spurs chairman Peter Holt said in Portland after the game. "I love you, San Antonio. San Antonio has truly been our sixth player."

Henry Williams, a sixth-grade teacher, has been a Spurs supporter since the team's arrival in town. Naturally, he's thrilled the Spurs finally made the finals.

"It's great. It couldn't happen to a better bunch of guys," Williams said. "It's great for everyone, the city and the whole community."

ENTHUSIASM

Fans of the San Antonio Spurs have waited the franchise's entire existence—26 years—for a championship. As the team advanced through the playoffs, fans grew understandably more excited with each win. When the team returned from Portland, they were greeted at the airport by approximately 3,500 fans, while more diehards camped out at the Alamodome to purchase NBA Finals tickets. Here, avid Spurs fans do their best to distract Latrell Sprewell at the free throw line.

MARIO ELIE AND TIM DUNCAN WATCH A SHOT IN PRACTICE BEFORE THE NBA FINALS.

SPURS MASTER THE WAITING GAME

BY KELLEY SHANNON   JUNE 8, 1999

SAN ANTONIO (AP)—David Robinson isn't worried about having more than a week off before the NBA Finals. He's getting used to these layoffs.

"We're just going to take a couple of days and get our minds right, get our bodies right and get ready to go," he said.

The San Antonio Spurs won their first trip to the championship round by sweeping the Portland Trail Blazers in the Western Conference finals with a 94-80 victory Sunday.

Now San Antonio awaits the outcome of the Eastern Conference finals, with Indiana and New York tied 2-2. The NBA Finals begin June 16 at the Alamodome.

Coach Gregg Popovich didn't schedule practices for Monday or Tuesday. Workouts resume Wednesday.

"The gym's locked," Popovich said. "We don't want to see them on the court. We just want them to mentally and physically just restore themselves a little bit."

Rust does not seem to be a big concern for the Spurs, especially for veterans like Robinson who are glad to have some time off.

"It's played well for us so far," said Robinson, pointing out the Spurs had a few days off between each playoff series this year.

The Spurs have swept their last two rounds 4-0 and have won 10 straight playoff games.

"After the first round we had a nice little rest then we came back pretty fresh. Five days, after the second round. But I think we'll do the same this time," Robinson said. "We'll be ready to go."

The time off also gives point guard Avery Johnson's left knee a chance to heal. He bruised it late in the first half of Sunday's game after he slipped on a wet spot. But Johnson came back to play most of the second half.

Popovich said there is nothing structurally wrong and the bruise will ease. After arriving from Portland, Johnson sounded ready to go.

"We have to practice even harder," he said. "We've still got one more goal."

> "WE'RE JUST GOING TO TAKE A COUPLE OF DAYS AND GET OUR MINDS RIGHT, GET OUR BODIES RIGHT AND GET READY TO GO."

SPURS ARE REALLY HOT TICKET

BY KELLEY SHANNON   JUNE 9, 1999

SAN ANTONIO (AP) — The Spurs are in the NBA Finals for the first time, and suddenly long lost friends are surfacing everywhere.

What do they want?

Tickets.

"Contrary to popular belief, we aren't ticket machines," forward Sean Elliott said. "For all the people out there that are going to call up other players for tickets: We don't have them."

The Spurs, who advanced to the championship round by defeating Portland 4-0 in the Western Conference finals, will have been off 10 days by the time the NBA Finals begin June 16.

San Antonio awaits the outcome of the Eastern Conference finals between Indiana and New York.

After two days off, the Spurs resumed practicing Wednesday. And there was lots of rough contact.

The players admit it's easy to get distracted with all the hoopla around town, and the requests from old friends and casual acquaintances.

"The finals tickets, you get a lot of people call," point guard Avery Johnson said. "But that's a good problem to have. I'm not dealing with it. I've got my assistant and my wife, they deal with it. The main thing is to stay focused."

Tim Duncan, who grew up in the Virgin Islands, said fans in his hometown of St. Croix are yearning to get in on the NBA Finals frenzy.

SEAN ELLIOTT AND OTHER SPURS PLAYERS RECEIVED NUMEROUS REQUESTS FOR FINALS TICKETS.

"Strangest request? A bunch of people from the Virgin Islands want to come down," he said. "Like a hundred and fifty of them."

Each Spurs player receives three tickets from the team. He can then can buy up to six more.

"I have guys calling, 'Can I get four? Can I get five? I need three, the best seats,'" Elliott said. "I go, 'Hey, wait a minute, just because I play doesn't mean I can just go get 20 seats.' It's unbelievable."

But Elliott would certainly rather be a ticket broker now than a television spectator.

"I remember this time last year sitting at home watching somebody else do it," he said. "And being pretty envious."

THE WAITING GAME

Since the Spurs had more than a week's wait after the Portland series, Coach Gregg Popovich gave his team two days off before resuming practices so players would have a chance to rest both physically and mentally. Above left, Sean Elliott (left), Tim Duncan (21) and Avery Johnson hold a strategy discussion. Above right, Johnson and Popovich watch Duncan as he prepares to put up a shot.

MARIO ELIE RAISES HIS ARMS IN CELEBRATION
FOLLOWING A SPURS VICTORY.

TEXANS GO WILD FOR SPURS, STARS

BY TROY GOODMAN   **JUNE 10, 1999**

With two Texas teams making it to their league championship series, Lone Star pride is in high gear this week.

Hockey fans and basketball devotees across the state are rallying around the Dallas Stars and San Antonio Spurs. It's a rare opportunity for everyone, including those from cities without their own teams, to get on the bandwagon.

One ebullient Dallas radio talk show host said Monday, "A Texas takeover—bring that on."

Merchandisers are adding staff, beefing up stock and doing what they can to get hockey and basketball team gear to thousands of souvenir-hungry fans.

"We've more than doubled the stock, and even that's not sufficient" said Terrence Brown of Aramark, a company licensed to the Spurs to sell official team products. "We've had to have everything expressed in (by shipping companies)."

Brown said the demand for merchandise specially made for the Western Conference champs has pushed sales about 40 percent higher for this time of year. Aramark has two stores—one inside the Alamodome and the other within walking distance of the stadium.

At the StarStuff store in the Dallas area, located at the Dr. Pepper Stars Center in suburban Irving, sales are running 300 percent above previous years.

Jill Moore, the Dallas Stars' retail manager, told *The Dallas Morning News:* "It's just nonstop. The frightening thing is this is nothing like what it will be if we win the Stanley Cup."

Both sports franchises sell traditional team-branded sports goods, like tee shirts, posters, jackets, caps and game jerseys. But the stores are also seeing a rush on newly minted souvenirs like miniature Stars goalie masks, matchbox-sized Zambonies, Spurs beer steins and silver and black Spurs car flags.

Brown said he's even considered stocking actual boot spurs, made of heavy metal with a Spurs logo branded on the cowboy gizmo's boot latch.

For their own part, San Antonio officials are expecting the benefits of a Spurs championship bid to bring in even more cash and more exposure that the city saw when it played host to the NCAA Final Four two years ago.

"Were excited to be going to the dance," said Carmen Vazquez-Gonzalez, a spokeswoman for the city manager's office. "The first two finals games are sold out, and this means (the city) gets much more international coverage—it's the NBA."

John Solis, of the San Antonio Convention and Visitors Bureau, said a Spurs championship could turn out to be the biggest event the city has played host to.

Lance Helgeson, managing editor for IEG Sponsorship Report, a newsletter that tracks national trends in marketing, said the championship series could enable the Stars and Spurs to earn $1 million to $2 million each from sponsors in future negotiations.

The immediate benefit, Helgeson said, is that car dealerships, fast food chains and other local businesses will want to have their names appearing next to the Stars and Spurs logos.

"That's the spillover effect," Helgeson said "You're going to have more people want to buy more stuff to be part of the action."

After 26 years of allegiance, Spurs fans have a reason to get excited about the possibility of a championship. Following the team's 4-0 sweep of the Portland Trail Blazers on Sunday, many camped out at the Alamodome to buy tickets for the NBA Finals.

Henry Williams, a San Antonio sixth-grade teacher and Spurs fan since the team came to town in 1973, has bought tickets for games from time to time. He said he managed to get tickets for some games in each playoff round this year.

"And the bank is broke," Williams said.

WADE ANDERSON PAINTS THE HALLWAY WALLS OF THE
ALAMODOME BEFORE THE NBA FINALS.

ANTICIPATION

Spurs fans have been waiting and hoping for a title for 26 years. Anticipation grew as the Spurs added one win after another to their postseason victory total. Three wins, then seven, then eleven took them to the Finals—just four victories away from bringing home the title. The fans weren't the only ones anticipating—David Robinson (left) celebrates the Spurs' win in Game 1 of the Western Conference Finals, while Tim Duncan (right) watches the action against the Portland Trail Blazers during Game 3.

COACH GREGG POPOVICH DIRECTS HIS TEAM DURING GAME 1 OF THE NBA FINALS.

SPURS' "POP" ENDURED TOUGH TIMES

BY KELLEY SHANNON   **JUNE 12, 1999**

SAN ANTONIO (AP)—Only three months ago, Gregg Popovich heard boos. Some fans wanted the coach fired.

Now the San Antonio Spurs are in the NBA Finals, and his critics are nowhere to be found. If Popovich takes private pleasure in the turn of events, he won't say so.

"It's not about vindication. It's about getting better. We started out poorly and we were a poor team. We continued to work. We got better and better," Popovich said.

San Antonio, after starting the season 6-8 in February, won 31 of its last 36 games and captured the Midwest Division and Western Conference titles. The top-seeded Spurs are 11-1 in the postseason, having swept their last two playoff opponents to reach the finals.

The Spurs will face the New York Knicks, who beat Indiana 90-82 in Game 6 Friday night. The finals begin Wednesday in San Antonio.

Popovich and his players say they don't think much about the team's miserable start.

"We probably thought about it more when we were 6-8, I would imagine. But that was a long time ago and a different team, really, as far as organization is concerned and our time together," Popovich said.

Perhaps the lowest point came February 28, when the Spurs were blown out on their home court by longtime nemesis Utah. Popovich was tossed from the game with two technicals in the third quarter, so he wasn't around for the end of the game and the boos from the Alamodome crowd.

Speculation intensified that Popovich would be ousted as coach.

"We weren't playing well. They were talking about Pop getting fired," guard Mario Elie said. "We weren't playing up to our capability."

David Robinson, who'd spent all 10 years of his professional career in San Antonio, even became the subject of trade rumors. Robinson said the Spurs players knew something had to change—and fast.

"At that point, you'd better figure out how to string together five or six wins in a row," Robinson said. "There were doubts. Everybody had doubts. We had to get through it."

Two nights after the Utah debacle, life improved for the Spurs with a victory at Houston. It was the start of a nine-game winning streak that set the tone for the rest of the season.

"We decided to come together instead of separate," Elie said. "You learn from that. When you start off tough, you grow as individuals and you grow as a team and you realize, hey, you have to do whatever it takes to help the team win."

Popovich said his only satisfaction comes in feeling happy for what his players accomplished.

"I'm proud of them for staying the course and working through the hard times to enjoy the good times," he said. "That's our job and the guys did it well."

Instead of listening to jeers, Popovich now finds himself surrounded by the "Go Spurs Go" chants of a town jubilant over the team's first trip to the finals in its 26-year history in San Antonio. Popovich's detractors, if still out there, are silent.

Popovich is completing his second full season as coach. He became the team's general manager in 1994 and took over the coaching job after firing Bob Hill in December 1996.

Because he's also the general manager, Popovich had the benefit of assembling the team he coaches.

Besides drafting top pick Tim Duncan in 1997—a "no brainer," as Popovich put it—he added veterans Elie, Steve Kerr and Jerome Kersey this season to give the Spurs more playoff and championship experience.

Reaching the finals feels good, Popovich admits.

"But there are a lot of people who could take this group to the finals," he said. "It's a hell of a group of guys."

EXPERIENCE

JEROME KERSEY, STEVE KERR

Are you experienced? It's an important question in San Antonio. One of the things Gregg Popovich has done since becoming both coach and general manager of the Spurs is add players with NBA playoff and championship experience to his roster. Among the veteran faces new to the Alamodome this year are Jerome Kersey (above chasing a loose ball after knocking it away from Denver guard Cory Alexander) and Steve Kerr (right, working on his free throws during a Spurs practice).

TIM DUNCAN HOLDS THE BALL OUT OF REACH OF NEW YORK'S LARRY JOHNSON.

TIM DUNCAN

BY JEANNINE RELLY   JUNE 16, 1999

CHRISTIANSTED, U.S. Virgin Islands (AP)—If Hurricane Hugo hadn't hit, Tim Duncan probably would be dreaming of Olympic gold as a swimmer, and the San Antonio Spurs might be just another team that's never made it to the NBA Finals.

But the hurricane that ravaged his native St. Croix in 1989 destroyed the only Olympic-sized pool. So the tallest teen-ager on the island turned to football, then basketball.

At first, he was so clumsy he was the butt of jokes.

"He never got angry, he'd just play harder," recalled former classmate Carl Hennemann, now an army lieutenant in Hawaii.

Duncan, coach Cuthbert George said, couldn't even dunk the ball.

"He was shy, very shy," George said. "I thought he wasn't aggressive enough to compete."

But he was a quick study, starting as a quarterback, and showed remarkable stamina that is attributed to his swimming background. He was a top U.S. competitor for his age group in the 400-meter freestyle.

Former coach Neville James noted that he always was "the perfect player, a team player. He didn't demand that he score all the time. He didn't have any ego."

Duncan soon sharpened his skills, and the gawky youth showed promise of the graceful jump hooks and slam dunks to come.

He carried The Demons of St. Dunstan's Episcopal High School to an undefeated season in 1992. The year before, The Demons had an 0-12 record.

He was an honor student, so bright he skipped third grade and graduated among the top five students, former headmistress Catherine Milligan-Terrell said.

But he also was something of a clown, joining classmates to run through the abandoned Salt River Hotel evading paint ball shots and, at least twice, playing truant for a day of bodysurfing at the beach.

The 7-footer was offered scholarships to Georgetown, Delaware and Providence. But he chose Wake Forest in North Carolina to study for a degree in psychology, perhaps because his sister lives in Winston-Salem.

After his sophomore and junior years, he turned down chances to enter the NBA draft to fulfill a promise to his mother that he would earn a degree. She died of cancer the day before the 23-year-old basketball star's 14th birthday.

The year after he earned his degree, the forward for the San Antonio Spurs was voted Rookie of the Year and an All-NBA first-team player, an honor he earned for the second time in 1999.

"I knew of him always as a quiet fire, a quiet giant. His laid-back attitude is the embodiment of people of St. Croix, doing things without fanfare and hoopla," said Senate President Vargrave Richards, whose daughter attended St. Dunstan's.

"He's an ideal role model for the youngsters," said Maria Heywood of the St. Croix federation of teachers. "He's humble and has a lot of principle. You can see he came from a traditional Virgin Islands upbringing."

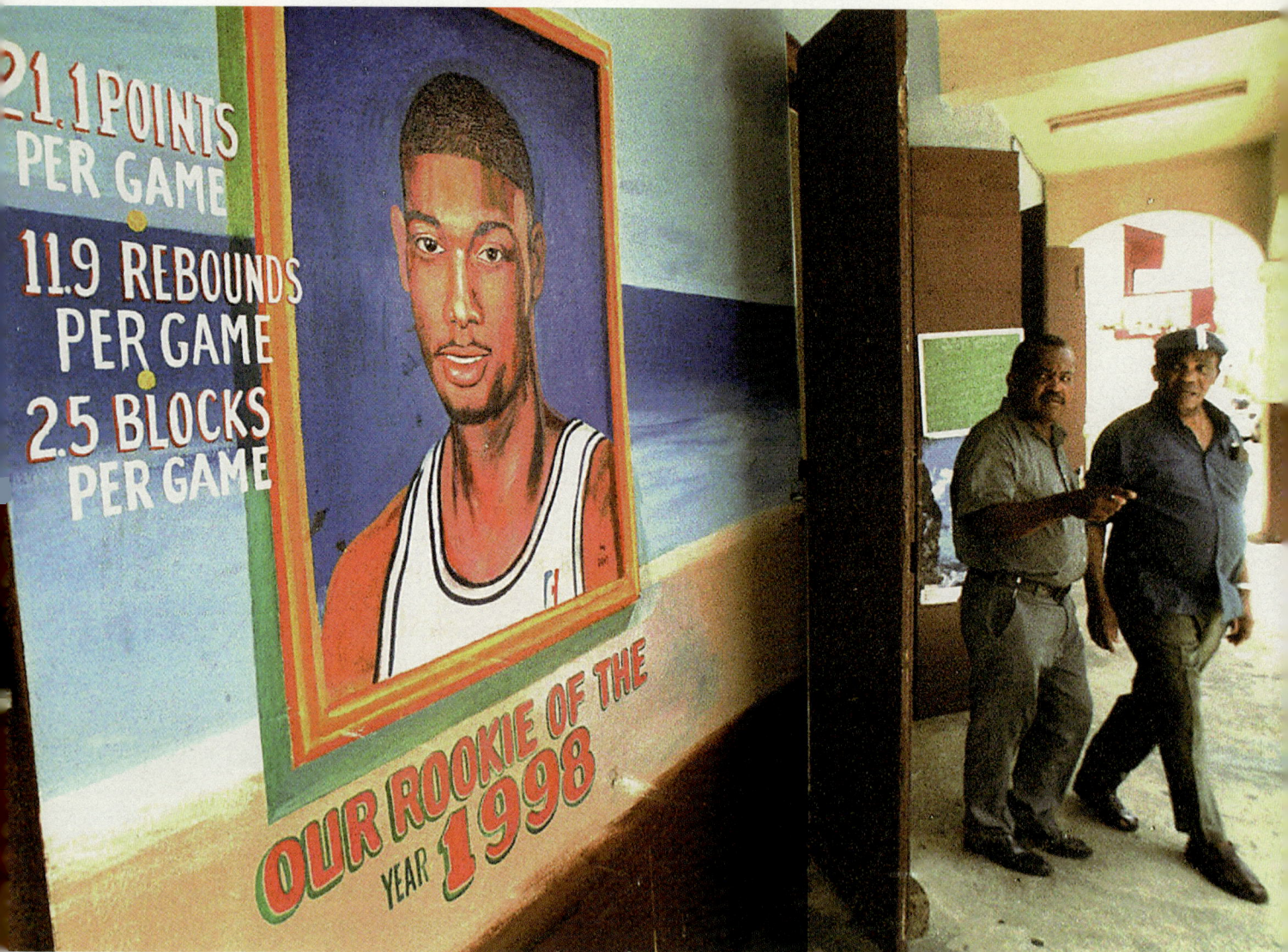

A MURAL HONORING TIM DUNCAN ADORNS HARVEY'S RESTAURANT IN ST. CROIX.

Duncan's fame has put St. Croix on the map, and islanders are returning the favor.

While St. Croix airport is being renovated, fans have erected a massive billboard photograph of the island's favorite son in the parking lot announcing: "Welcome to St. Croix—Home of Tim Duncan."

The cash-strapped government hopes to make money from him and is discussing giving a 100 percent tax break to his T.D. Enterprises, which plans several ventures, including a sports bar in St. Croix.

A new high school gym has been named after him, with every wall plastered with pictures of the school's barracuda mascot decked out in No. 21 gear.

A mural of his face headlined "Our Rookie of the Year" graces the front wall of Harvey's Restaurant, and inside there's a photo gallery. Harvey's has erected a huge TV screen for fans wanting to see Duncan lead the Spurs in the Alamodome in San Antonio for the start of the NBA Finals.

Wednesday afternoon, some 150 islanders boarded a charter jet bound for the finals. Seeing them off was Pamela Richards, the acting commissioner of tourism, who said Duncan's fame had promoted the Virgin Islands more than any advertising the government could dream of buying.

"Timmy has placed St. Croix on the map and we are eternally grateful for that," she said.

THE TWIN TOWERS

TIM DUNCAN, DAVID ROBINSON

When the Spurs drafted Tim Duncan in 1997, David Robinson worked out with the eventual Rookie of the Year before the season even began. Since then, with Robinson adjusting his role to take advantage of his young teammate's talents, the two 7-footers have become the latest wonder of the world—The Twin Towers. Duncan shines in the offense, as shown above versus New York's Chris Dudley, while Robinson (right, blocking a shot by Joe Smith of the Minnesota Timberwolves) has assumed an even greater leadership role on the defensive end.

AVERY JOHNSON POINTS TO THE SPURS' BENCH
DURING SAN ANTONIO'S 89-77 VICTORY OVER
NEW YORK IN GAME 1 OF THE NBA FINALS.

GAME 1

SPURS 89, KNICKS 77

BY KEN BERGER   JUNE 17, 1999

SAN ANTONIO (AP)—Tim Duncan seemed to grasp this moment as well as anyone his age possibly could.

After dicing up the New York Knicks with an array of layups and bank shots, Duncan even tried to be funny. Informed that several former Spurs were on hand to watch the franchise's first game in the NBA Finals, Duncan loosened up and said, "I didn't even know they were here. But yeah, I was playing for them."

That's it, polish your image, young man. This ride might just be starting.

With an effort that was efficient, effective and deceptively ruthless, Duncan and the San Antonio Spurs beat the New York Knicks 89-77 Wednesday night to take a 1-0 lead in the NBA Finals.

Duncan, who had 33 points and 16 rebounds, seemed to recognize that nearly all that needed fixing about him was his sense of humor. Great moves, dull quotes is the book on the 23-year-old Duncan.

His artistry and persistence around the basket were far more impressive than his jokes.

The Knicks had no answer whatsoever for Duncan and his 7-foot counterpart, David Robinson. Every time they made a run, they were jolted back to reality by a clutch shot from Jaren Jackson.

Robinson had 13 points, nine rebounds and seven assists. Jackson had 17 points, including five 3-pointers that stole all the steam from the Knicks' dogged comebacks in front of a crowd of nearly 40,000—the second-largest in the history of the finals.

The biggest dagger from Jackson came with 8:10 left as he was falling out of bounds right in front of the Knicks' sideline. That shot made it 77-68 after New York closed within six points. It was the Knicks' last stand in the Alamodome.

"A couple of shots, like the one out of bounds, I think the (shot) clock was going down," Jackson said. "I'm glad I was just hitting some of those."

So are the Spurs, who won their 11th straight playoff game to tie an NBA record. In stopping the Knicks from making one of their thrilling final pushes down the stretch, the Spurs became the first team to

> THE KNICKS HAD NO ANSWER WHATSOEVER FOR DUNCAN AND HIS 7-FOOT COUNTERPART, DAVID ROBINSON. EVERY TIME THEY MADE A RUN, THEY WERE JOLTED BACK TO REALITY BY A CLUTCH SHOT FROM JAREN JACKSON.

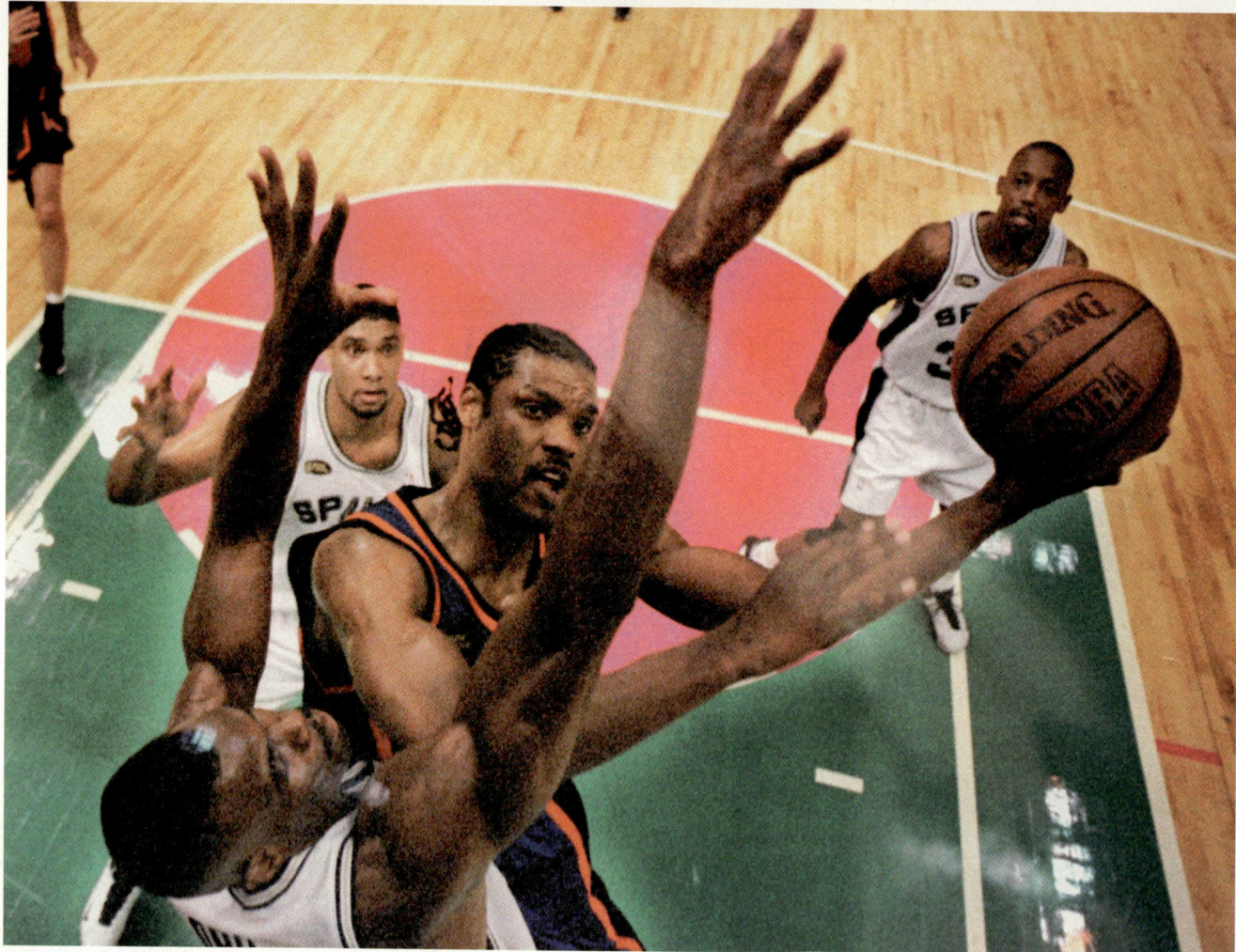

LATRELL SPREWELL ATTEMPTS A SHOT OVER DAVID ROBINSON DURING GAME 1 OF THE NBA FINALS.

keep the Knicks from winning the first game of a series in these playoffs.

"It's been a fun ride so far," said Robinson, eerily speaking as though the Spurs' final goal is not that far off. "We just know we're a 48-minute, grind-it-out kind of team. We just know we're not going anywhere. We just keep grinding, keep working."

"We were there. We were right there, that's the one thing I'll say," Latrell Sprewell said. "You look at how many guys they had that played well and we're only 8-10 points out of it, if we can just take away a few of those 3s and a few of those postups, this might have been different."

Easier said than done when Messrs Robinson and Duncan are doing their dirty work.

Robinson passed to Duncan from the high post with devastating results, blocked three shots and altered several others. Duncan scored on seven jumpers and six layups, shooting 13-for-21. He scored three baskets during an 11-4 run as the Spurs asserted their dominance in the third quarter, then scored three more after Jackson's 3-pointer buried the Knicks in the fourth.

"It wasn't easy at all," said Duncan, his statement defying reality. "I worked hard tonight. I really did."

Van Gundy, who escaped his seemingly certain firing during the eighth-seeded Knicks' improbable journey to the finals, has quite an off day ahead of him.

"We've got to take away Jaren Jackson," Van Gundy said. "Obviously, Duncan's going to score. We've got to take everything else away."

FRUSTRATION

Some days it just doesn't pay to get out of bed in the morning. The Spurs frustrated the Knicks at every turn in Game 1 of the NBA Finals, winning by a final score of 89-77 in San Antonio. While Spurs fans continued to look forward to a championship, Knicks coach Jeff Van Gundy (left), master of surprises, was left to ponder his next move. Knicks fan Lori Maloney, watching the live telecast of the game at Madison Square Garden, buried her face in her Knicks towel.

JAREN JACKSON (LEFT), THE HERO OF GAME 1, AND JEROME KERSEY ENJOY THE ACTION FROM THE BENCH.

JACKSON FINDS NICHE IN SAN ANTONIO

BY KELLEY SHANNON   **JUNE 17, 1999**

SAN ANTONIO (AP)—Jaren Jackson is no stranger to the back roads of the CBA or the benches of the NBA.

Jackson played for the Wichita Falls Texans and the La Crosse Catbirds. He was cut by the New Jersey Nets during a road trip. He did a brief stint in France, where he struggled to speak French.

A journeyman willing to go wherever his love for basketball takes him, the San Antonio Spurs guard looks fondly upon the lessons he's learned as a traveling man.

"Always have a nice luggage set," Jackson said. "I've been to the little towns and the big cities."

Now as a trusted reserve for the Spurs, Jackson has found some career stability. He's provided San Antonio with solid shooting in the playoffs and was a key to the Spurs' 89-77 victory over the New York Knicks in Game 1 of the NBA Finals.

Knicks coach Jeff Van Gundy said Jackson's 17 points, including five 3-pointers, hurt New York more than Tim Duncan's 33 points Wednesday. Duncan is expected to have a big game. But Van Gundy doesn't want to let the Spurs' supporting players do the same.

"We've got to find a way to keep the other guys out of the game. We did that with some of the guys. We didn't do a good enough job on Jaren Jackson," Van Gundy said.

Jackson joined the Spurs before the 1997-98 season after having played for seven other NBA teams. He played college basketball at Georgetown, graduating in 1989.

Jackson wasn't drafted by an NBA team. New Jersey signed him as a free agent shortly after college and waived him a few months later. Then he played in the Continental Basketball Association with Wichita Falls in Texas and La Crosse in Wisconsin, winning a championship with each team.

He also played in Pittsburgh and Fort Wayne, Indiana, in the CBA and for the Dayton Wings in Ohio in the WBL, a small summer league.

Once he established himself in the minor leagues, Jackson began to land contracts in the NBA. He played for Golden State, Portland, Philadelphia, Houston, Washington and the Los Angeles Clippers. He was signed by Chicago before the 1993-94 season, but was waived before the regular season.

Jackson and fellow Spurs guards Mario Elie and Avery Johnson often joke about their lengthy resumes.

"Everybody knows the story about how A.J. was cut by the Spurs once, the Spurs twice. We try to joke about that moment when the coach is telling you you're gone," he said. "If it happens, you've got to move on."

Spurs coach Gregg Popovich said he's thrilled for Jackson that the situation in San Antonio has worked out.

"You have to respect the fact that he continued, that he never stopped trying to get it right," Popovich said.

If basketball hadn't been an option, Jackson said, he never doubted he could make a living in the "real world." He earned a degree in finance. His wife, Terri, also a Georgetown graduate, is a lawyer. An avid reader, Jackson said he enjoyed school and that he would like to eventually return for more education.

He always dreamed of playing in the NBA.

"Deep down, I've always felt that I can play in this league just as well as any of these guys," Jackson said. "Even through all those times of getting cut, you just have to believe it."

Jackson, who becomes a free agent after this season, said he enjoys San Antonio and finally feels at home.

"But I did feel a little bit that way in Washington. I felt a little bit that way in other places, too," he cautioned.

For now, Jackson is concentrating on helping the Spurs win a championship. Whether he has a future with the Spurs isn't definite.

As always, his luggage is waiting.

"I'm keeping the situation with a level head, not too overconfident," he said. "I'm not going to count my chickens yet."

RESERVE JAREN JACKSON TURNED IN AN OUTSTANDING OFFENSIVE PERFORMANCE AGAINST THE KNICKS IN GAME 1.

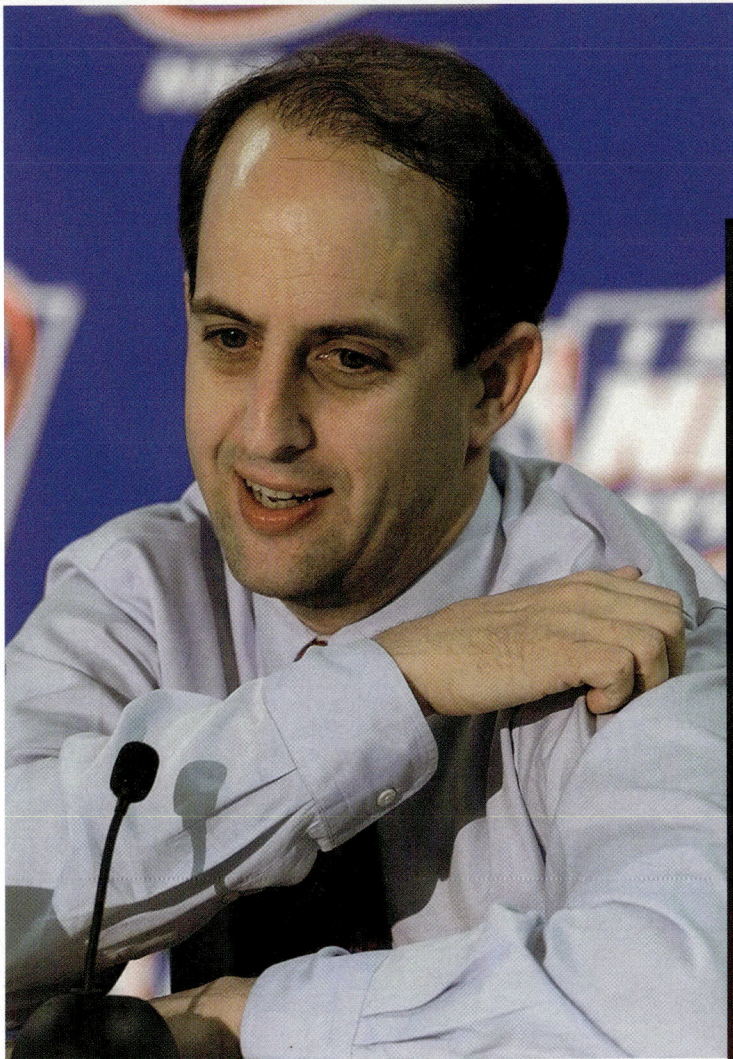

THE COACHES

JEFF VAN GUNDY, GREGG POPOVICH

Gregg Popovich likes to say he is the only NBA coach with a lower profile than Jeff Van Gundy. This season, both coaches have had to deal with their share of negative attention. When the Spurs opened the season 6-8, many fans in San Antonio were calling for Popovich to be fired. Van Gundy had to deal with his normal trials and tribulations, as well as a variety of rumors about whether Dave Checketts was planning to replace him with Phil Jackson. In the end, both coaches managed to quiet the critics by leading their teams to the NBA Finals.

AVERY JOHNSON AND TIM DUNCAN HUG TO CEL-
EBRATE THE SPURS' GAME 2 VICTORY OVER THE
KNICKS.

SPURS WANT POSTSEASON WIN RECORD

BY CHRIS SHERIDAN   JUNE 17, 1999

SAN ANTONIO (AP)—The San Antonio Spurs have a chance to do something that the greatest teams in NBA history—even Bill Russell's Boston Celtics and Michael Jordan's Chicago Bulls—never accomplished: 12 consecutive postseason victories.

And on the day between Games 1 and 2 of the NBA Finals, they couldn't have cared less.

"That playoff winning streak record is not important whatsoever," Spurs center David Robinson said Thursday. "Nobody in our locker room has talked about it or even cared about it."

The Spurs were more concerned about maintaining their mental edge and staying hungry for Game 2 Friday night against the New York Knicks.

Their Game 1 victory was a product of the same winning formula they've used all year: plenty of production from Tim Duncan; support on offense and defense from Robinson; timely shooting by one of their outside specialists, in this case Jaren Jackson.

Despite an 11-game winning streak, the Spurs have run into trouble in Game 2s during each of their playoff series. In the first round, they lost to Minnesota. In the second round, they needed two late missed free throws by Kobe Bryant to beat the Los Angeles Lakers. In the third round, they trailed Portland by 18 before winning on Sean Elliott's incredible tippy-toe 3-pointer.

"It's not just this team, it's any team," said Steve Kerr, a veteran of three NBA Finals with the Bulls. "You see a team win Game 1 in the finals and there's a natural tendency to let down a little bit. The other team is angry and comes out and plays a lot better, and all of a sudden it's 1-1.

"We've had some trouble in Game 2s, so it'll be important for us to come out strong early."

In Game 1, it was the Knicks who came out strong, only to falter in the second quarter when they got into foul trouble. New York was still within striking distance, trailing by six early in the fourth quarter, but Jackson's two big 3-pointers deflated the Knicks.

Jackson, who had five 3-pointers in scoring 17 points, was the one player who ruined the Knicks' strategy of letting Duncan get his points while trying to contain everyone else.

The Knicks used to use the same strategy against Jordan, although it usually came up short then, too.

Duncan said the only thing about the Knicks' defense that surprised him was that he wasn't immediately double-teamed in the low post. Sometimes the Knicks used one defender, and other times waited until Duncan dribbled before sending reinforcements.

"We don't really like to double, we prefer to play straight up," New York's Kurt Thomas said. "But we're going to have to double at times and mix it up. If we don't double him, he might get 60."

"I don't think demoralized would be the right word. Obviously they were disappointed and discouraged," Robinson said. "They really brought their 'A' game, they were genuinely excited. With the way we fought back, I think they were a little surprised that we were able to take over the game like that."

"The problem with San Antonio is you may get by the first shot blocker, but then there's the next shot blocker. It's very difficult to get quality shots," Van Gundy said.

San Antonio is tied with the 1988-89 Los Angeles Lakers for the longest playoff winning streak for one season, and Friday will mark the 38th day since the Spurs last lost a game.

Kerr said he wouldn't pick these Spurs over last year's Bulls, even though he is impressed by this long run of victories.

"With the Bulls, we won eight or nine in a row a couple of times," Kerr said, "but this is as good a roll as there's ever been in this league.

"Out of those 11 games, there were two of them that we got a little lucky with. So, yeah, we got a couple of breaks, but that's part of the game."

KNICKS FANS CHEER AS THEIR TEAM TAKES THE COURT IN SAN ANTONIO.

SWEEP?

Instead of sugarplums, Spurs fans had visions of brooms dancing in their heads. After sweeping the Lakers in the second round of the playoffs and the Trail Blazers in the Western Conference Finals, the Spurs had a chance at an amazing accomplishment— 12 straight postseason victories. They set the record by winning Game 2 of the NBA Finals, leading some fans to predict a sweep of the Knicks and an unprecedented 14 consecutive playoff victories, but were foiled by the Knicks' victory in Game 3. Above, Mario Elie battles Rasheed Wallace (left), Brian Grant and Damon Stoudamire of Portland. At right, Malik Rose fouls the Lakers' Kobe Bryant as Bryant goes for a layup.

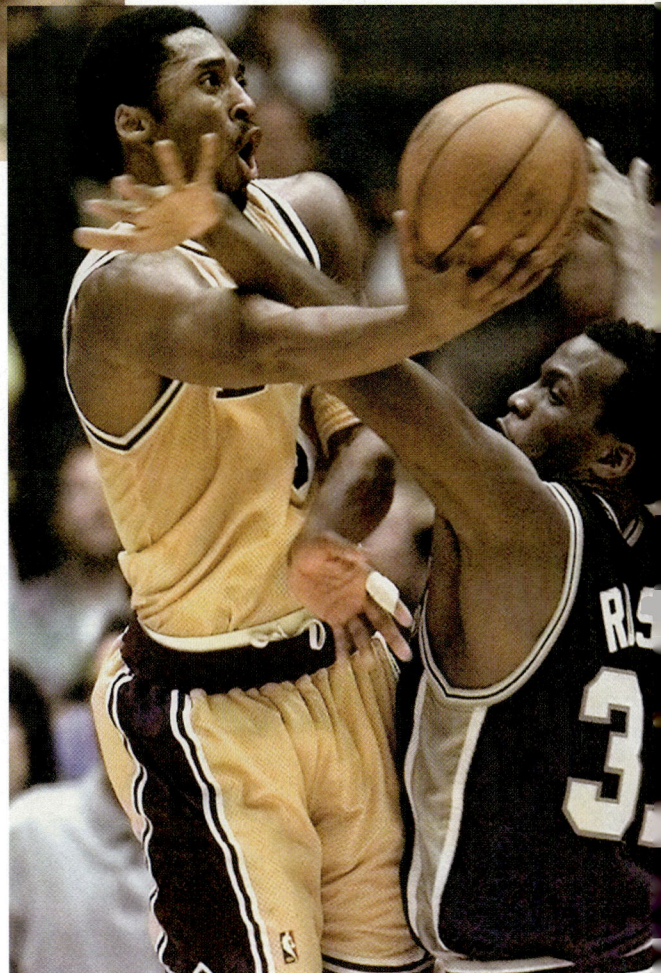

MARIO ELIE GETS OFF A PASS WHILE BEING GUARDED BY
KNICKS CENTER CHRIS DUDLEY.

GAME 2

SPURS 80, KNICKS 67

BY KEN BERGER   JUNE 19, 1999

SAN ANTONIO (AP)—David Robinson hugged his little friend, Avery Johnson. Tim Duncan checked out to a standing ovation, too, as chants for a sweep filled the Alamodome.

Despite taking a 2-0 lead in the NBA Finals with a record-setting victory, the San Antonio Spurs had to admit they were just a little embarrassed by how they got there.

Though they failed to dominate the hobbling, abysmally shooting New York Knicks, the Spurs nonetheless beat them 80-67 Friday night to move within two games of a sweep in the finals. They extended their playoff winning streak to 12 games, the longest in one postseason in the NBA's 52-year history. The Los Angeles Lakers won 11 straight games in the 1988 playoffs.

The Spurs broke that mark without much artistry, amid a clank-filled shooting performance by the Knicks.

"It was a very ugly win. No way to hide that," said Duncan, who once again led the Spurs with 25 points, 15 rebounds and four blocks. "But we win best when it's ugly. We can pull those types of games out."

Until Jaren Jackson hit a 3-pointer with 10.1 seconds left and the Knicks scored a meaningless basket at the buzzer, the teams were on track to shatter the record-low of 145 combined points set by Syracuse and Fort Wayne in 1955.

The Knicks shot 33 percent and needed 82 shots to score 67 points. Latrell Sprewell and Allan Houston put up 42 of those. Sprewell had 26 points on 8-for-22 shooting, while Houston shot 9-for-20 for 19 points.

"We're getting shots," Sprewell said. "We're just not making them."

Knicks coach Jeff Van Gundy observed, "Obviously, I don't think we're playing well offensively."

"The guys are obviously disappointed," Sprewell said. "This is not the position we wanted to be in."

If the Spurs continue their composed march, they have a chance to set the record for winning percentage in a postseason. The Spurs are 13-1, their only loss coming in Game 2 of their first-round series against Minnesota at home.

The record belongs to the 1983 Philadelphia 76ers, who were 12-1 in winning a championship. The best record since the league went to 15 wins needed for the title is shared by the 1989 Detroit Pistons and 1991 Chicago Bulls—both 15-2.

"We are not going to blow guys out," said Robinson, who had another efficient night's work with 16 points on 5-for-8 shooting, 11 rebounds and five blocks. "You look up at the clock in the first half, and they're shooting 28 percent, 30 percent. You feel like you should be up by 15.

"You just can't press yourself. Steady, 48 minutes, play your game."

TIM DUNCAN JOGS DOWN THE COURT AT THE ALAMODOME.

The Knicks' shooting woes were never worse than in the fourth quarter, when they went nearly seven minutes without a field goal. The drought was epitomized by a shot from Houston that bounced off the shot clock as it expired.

Sprewell finally broke the field-goal drought on a jumper with 1:32 left, but Duncan answered right away with an alley-oop dunk that made it 71-61 and led to chants of "Sweep, Sweep" from the Alamodome crowd of 39,554—the second-largest in finals history.

"Sweep is not something that ever went through our minds in L.A. or Portland, very honestly," Spurs coach Gregg Popovich said. "It was the furthest thing from our minds.

"With this group of guys, they don't need any speeches from me. They know what the deal is."

PERSEVERANCE

SEAN ELLIOTT

You don't become a force in the NBA without perseverance. The Spurs have that quality in abundance. Avery Johnson, Jaren Jackson and Mario Elie have shown it throughout their careers as they bounced from team to team. The team has demonstrated it since they began pulling together, rather than apart, after a rocky start to the season. And Sean Elliott has shown it by overcoming an injury-plagued 1997-98 season to become a consistent outside threat for the Spurs. Here, Elliott's perseverance is clear as he battles Bryon Russell of the Jazz (left) and Charlie Ward of the Knicks (right) for loose balls.

DAVID ROBINSON BLOCKS JERMAINE O'NEAL'S SHOT
DURING GAME 3 OF THE WESTERN CONFERENCE
FINALS.

ROBINSON DOESN'T MIND SECONDARY ROLE

BY KELLEY SHANNON   JUNE 19, 1999

SAN ANTONIO (AP—Playing a secondary role to a second-year pro wouldn't appeal to many veteran stars.

David Robinson doesn't seem to mind, especially if teaming with Tim Duncan helps the San Antonio Spurs win an NBA championship.

"When he came to San Antonio, when we first drafted him, I didn't know the extent of what his talents were," Robinson said. He found out quickly what the top draft pick could do.

The two 7-footers worked out together during the summer of 1997 before Duncan's rookie season in what Robinson describes as "a good, positive competitiveness." They've built on that foundation since.

In the Spurs' first trip to the NBA Finals, San Antonio rode the Duncan-Robinson duo to consecutive victories over the New York Knicks. The best-of-7 series shifts to Madison Square Garden for Game 3 Monday night.

So far, Robinson has found the finals a blast.

"I think winning makes a big difference in the fun factor," he said. "Everybody works hard. This is when it all pays off."

Knicks coach Jeff Van Gundy said Robinson and Duncan make each shot in the paint difficult.

"They're a great defensive team," Van Gundy said. "At the basket, they're terrific. Nothing comes easy with those two guys in there."

Defensive leadership has been Robinson's main job this season, while the Spurs have made Duncan their chief offensive weapon.

"Tim is the guy we go to, and we go to him down the stretch quite a bit," Robinson said. "A lot of that pressure is off me now."

But offensive aggressiveness is still part of Robinson's game, especially in the fourth quarter when the game is at a pivotal point.

After the Knicks closed within 63-57 with 7:55 left Friday night, Robinson responded with a slam dunk, then hit a 17-foot jumper less than 30 seconds later, giving San Antonio a 10-point lead.

That was the end for New York.

Robinson's somewhat reduced role runs counter to what he'd become used to most of his 10 years in the league. Robinson was the top draft pick in 1987 and joined the Spurs two years later following a Navy commitment.

Robinson essentially became the Spurs franchise. He was Rookie of the Year in the 1989-90 season. He won the NBA rebounding title in 1991, the blocked shots title in 1992, the scoring

title in 1994 and was chosen Most Valuable Player in 1995.

The rub on Robinson was that he was "soft," that he couldn't follow through on his regular-season success with a strong postseason performance.

Robinson contended he needed a little help, that he couldn't do it alone. This season he's gotten the assistance he's craved from Duncan, plus a healthy Sean Elliott, an improved Avery Johnson and the addition of playoff veteran Mario Elie.

Now Robinson is two victories away from a championship.

"You can't prove it until you actually win," he said, "but finally it's coming together."

DAVID ROBINSON JR. HANGS OUT WITH HIS DAD DURING A SPURS PRACTICE IN SAN ANTONIO.

DEFENSE

TIM DUNCAN, SEAN ELLIOTT

The Chicago Bulls preached it after winning each of their six championship trophies, and everyone says it—defense wins championships. The Spurs took the adage to heart, as their opponents had the lowest field goal percentage in the NBA. They also led the league in blocked shots while finishing third in points allowed and fourth in rebounds. Tim Duncan, shown above left blocking Vlade Divac, finished fifth in the league in blocked shots, with David Robinson close behind in seventh. Above right, Sean Elliott puts pressure on the Mavericks' Dirk Nowitzki.

Avery Johnson attempts to pass the ball under pressure from Shawn Bradley (center) and Steve Nash of the Dallas Mavericks.

AVERY JOHNSON KNOWS ABOUT TRAVELING

BY HAL BOCK   JUNE 20, 1999

NEW YORK (AP)—As many places as he's been and as many times as he's had to move, Avery Johnson plays basketball with a basic sense of insecurity.

He's not a franchise player like Tim Duncan or David Robinson, each a 7-footer, each able to dominate games with brute strength.

Instead, he's a journeyman point guard two wins from an NBA championship. Johnson is coach Gregg Popovich's on-court presence for the San Antonio Spurs.

"I always feel I'm one step from being cut," Johnson said Sunday. "Pop might wake up one day and say, 'We don't want you anymore.' That keeps you humble."

And that's a permanent state of mind for the guy with the high-pitched voice who's been playing the point in the NBA for 11 years after not even being drafted out of college.

This is the third time Johnson's NBA odyssey has passed through San Antonio. The other stops were in Seattle, where he signed originally as an undrafted free agent in 1988, Denver, Houston and Golden State. He even spent time in the U.S. Basketball League with the long-forgotten Palm Beach Stingrays.

He once was traded by Seattle for a second-round draft pick in a league where only the first-round picks usually mean anything. And the SuperSonics had to wait seven years to collect the draft choice.

He's been waived twice and signed as a free agent seven times. He has, as they say, been around the block.

"Some guys get older and worse," he said. "I got older and better.

"I'm a cerebral player in a lot of ways. The game is mental for me, not physical anymore. I'm not a 150-pound guy out of Southern University anymore.

"The only way to measure how good I am is by wins."

And the Spurs won more games than anybody else in the league this season, with Johnson averaging 9.7 points and 7.4 assists and keeping the big guys underneath happy.

"With Tim and Dave, I'm always mindful of their shot attempts," he said. "If I have to force the issue, I'll pass up the shot to get them the ball. You've got to keep Dave involved or he tends to float a little."

> "I ALWAYS FEEL I'M ONE STEP FROM BEING CUT," JOHNSON SAID SUNDAY. "POP MIGHT WAKE UP ONE DAY AND SAY, 'WE DON'T WANT YOU ANYMORE.' THAT KEEPS YOU HUMBLE."

**AVERY JOHNSON BATTLES UTAH'S KARL MALONE FOR THE
BALL WHILE JOHN STOCKTON LOOKS ON.**

If that sounds a little critical, it's not unusual. Johnson speaks his mind and on his mind is how the Spurs, flirting with all kinds of playoff records for wins, are playing right now.

"Our offense has not been good," he said, shaking his head. "Our spacing, our passing. We're passing when we shouldn't be and not passing when we should. We're not close to being good offensively."

Johnson has played well, with 14 points and 13 assists in the first two wins. He thinks he can turn his game up even further.

"When I don't have control and we make too many empty passes and shot clock violations, that's bad," he said. "We've got to do a better job."

And yet, they continue to win.

Johnson is 34 and brings maturity to a lineup where 23-year-old Tim Duncan has become the main man. AJ watches Duncan's approach to the postseason with some interest.

"Tim is excited," he said. "But our appreciation level is different because our frame of reference is different."

Duncan, remember, was a lottery player, the No. 1 pick in the draft. He didn't have to go shopping for a team. And he'll never be traded for a second-round pick.

And the Palm Beach Stingrays?

No chance.

QUESTIONS

Everybody has questions, and the public has a right to know—especially when you're in the NBA Finals. As the playoffs progress, the number of reporters covering the games also increases. They know who, when and where, but it's up to the participants to supply what, why and how. Here, David Robinson talks with the media at a practice in San Antonio.

KNICKS TEAMMATES
ALLAN HOUSTON AND
LATRELL SPREWELL
HUG AFTER DEFEATING
THE SPURS IN GAME 3
OF THE NBA FINALS.

GAME 3

KNICKS 89, SPURS 81

BY KEN BERGER   JUNE 22, 1999

NEW YORK (AP)—Brooms are now back in their closets all over San Antonio. The NBA Finals are a real series.

With a convincing victory in Game 3, the New York Knicks shattered the Spurs' invincible aura and perhaps rescued a series that seemed all but decided and anything but intriguing when it arrived at Madison Square Garden.

The Knicks beat the Spurs 89-81 Monday night with yet another lineup change and 34 points from Allan Houston, pulling to 2-1 in the best-of-7 series. For one thrilling night, the sound of remote controls clicking across America was drowned out by signs of life at the Garden.

Notice to those who jammed San Antonio's streets in a broom-waving traffic jam only three nights ago: We may have ourselves a series, after all.

"It's always been a series," said Marcus Camby, who didn't do much with his first start for the Knicks until he threw down a thunderous dunk in the fourth quarter. "The only thing San Antonio did down there was solidify home court. You're supposed to win on your home court. Now, they just put the emphasis on us. We have three games at the Garden."

That is a certainty now as Houston had one of the best games of his career and the Knicks did justice to the building Michael Jordan used to call "The Mecca of Basketball."

The Garden was nothing but a menace to the Spurs, who lost for the first time in 41 days. Tim Duncan had his worst game of the series, scoring 20 points, but getting shut out on 0-for-4 shooting in the fourth quarter.

Aside from David Robinson's 25 points and 10 rebounds, Duncan didn't get much help as San Antonio saw its NBA-record 12-game winning streak in these playoffs come to an end. It was the Spurs' first loss since dropping Game 2 to Minnesota in the first round on May 11, and their first after six consecutive road victories.

It was the first time in the series that the Knicks shot more free throws than the Spurs. New York was 23-for-30, and the Spurs 18-for-22. Duncan was only 4-for-4. In Games 1 and 2, the Spurs shot 66 foul shots to the Knicks' 31.

"I don't know what you'd call this tonight," Robinson said. "Our team absolutely hates to lose, and we always respond well after a loss. Always. Hopefully, guys are going to take this personally and come back with some more focus and energy on Wednesday."

That is when the Spurs, the Knicks and the formerly comatose finals return to the Garden for an intriguing game that will go a long way toward determining the first NBA champion of the post-Jordan, post-Bulls dynasty era. After TV ratings for Games 1 and 2 were down drastically from last season, maybe more will watch now.

"You saw the true character of the Knicks," New York coach Jeff Van Gundy said. "We hung in there when they were making runs, and we were very resilient."

Houston was 10-for-24 from the field in an electrifying performance that included a 3-pointer that broke the only tie of the game as the shot clock expired in the third. New York stopped every Spurs comeback, refusing to give them the lead after the Knicks opened a 14-point advantage in an explosive first quarter.

The Spurs got within one point near the end of the third and cut the deficit to 81-77 on Sean Elliott's 3-pointer with 3:13 left in the fourth. But Camby, who soared for a tremendous dunk on an offensive rebound for his first points early in the fourth, followed Houston's jumper with an 11-footer that gave New York an 85-77 lead with 2:20 left.

The Spurs cut it six points twice—on a running one-hander by Elliott and a free throw by Robinson—but that was all.

REFEREE DICK BAVETTA SEPARATES MARCUS CAMBY AND DAVID ROBINSON DURING A SCUFFLE IN THE THIRD QUARTER OF GAME 3.

Duncan, suddenly tentative in the post after two dominant games, passed to Mario Elie and then got the ball back, only to toss up an errant 3-pointer that would have cut it to 88-84 if it hadn't clunked off the front rim.

"It was just a stupid play," said Duncan, realizing that he should have shot the ball when he was closer to the basket. "I should have turned around and shot the ball. I made the wrong decision."

New York's Larry Johnson, who deserved much of the credit for containing Duncan, scored 16 points himself despite his ongoing battle with a sprained knee.

"We showed a lot of heart and character," Johnson said. "This is the NBA Finals. There isn't any lay-down-and-quit in this team. We are still in this."

ON THE SIDELINES

PATRICK EWING, SPIKE LEE

The Knicks fill the courtside seats of Madison Square Garden with famous fans, but perhaps none is more vocal than filmmaker Spike Lee (right), who seems to enjoy antagonizing opposing players as much as he does cheering on the Knicks. With his Knicks finally in the NBA Finals, Lee didn't miss the chance to show his support. Another famous face on the sidelines for the Finals is Patrick Ewing (above), whose playoff run was ended by a tear in his Achilles tendon. As the games go on without him, Ewing has implored his teammates to "get me my ring."

SEAN ELLIOTT (32) AND TIM DUNCAN (21) DEFEND LARRY JOHNSON AS HE LOOKS TO PUT UP A SHOT IN GAME 4 OF THE NBA FINALS.

GAME 4

SPURS 96, KNICKS 89

BY KEN BERGER   JUNE 22, 1999

NEW YORK (AP)—The San Antonio Spurs played like a championship team, with the emphasis on team.

For a change, the Twin Towers didn't stand alone.

With plenty of help for 7-footers Tim Duncan and David Robinson, the Spurs rediscovered their road magic Wednesday night with a 96-89 victory over the New York Knicks in Game 4 of the NBA Finals. They took a 3-1 lead in the best-of-7 series, a lead no team has ever relinquished in the final round.

From the shortest man on the court—Avery Johnson—all the way to Duncan and Robinson, the Spurs played like a team that is no longer content to stand around and wait for the 7-footers to carry them.

Now the Spurs have three chances to win one more time and give San Antonio its first NBA title.

"We have an opportunity to do something special, first time in San Antonio," said Mario Elie, who scored 18 points. "Hopefully, we can finish it off."

Duncan followed his worst game of the finals with a 28-point, 18-rebound performance. Robinson had 14 points and 17 rebounds, nine of them at the offensive end for the Spurs, who refused to let their six-game playoff winning streak on the road turn into a two-game losing streak.

Instead of standing back and admiring the big guys, Elie, Johnson and Sean Elliott were there to make whatever shots, steals, rebounds or passes the Spurs needed to keep the resilient Knicks coming back and tying the series.

Knicks coach Jeff Van Gundy said, "Size does matter in this league."

Not on this night. Not to the Spurs, and not during the crucial final moments of what the Knicks tried to turn into one of the biggest victories ever recorded in Madison Square Garden.

Instead, it turned into one giant step for the Spurs and another disappointment to add to the Knicks' postseason lore.

"This is the ultimate challenge," said New York's Allan Houston, who scored 20 points, but had three of the Knicks' 11 misses as they got within two points, but no closer, in the final 5 1/2 minutes. "Our backs can't be any further against the wall than when you're down 3-1 in the finals."

The Spurs beat the Knicks in every way possible, whether it was Duncan with his back to the basket, Robinson soaring above the rim or Elie throwing down a dunk and talking trash with Spike Lee.

"Toughness, man. That's what New York City ball's all about," said Elie, who recovered from a terrible Game 3 and shot 6-for-9 in the arena that is five minutes from where he grew up. "Going to the basket hard, finishing the play, dunking on people and talking trash. That's New York City ball."

Elliott had 14 points, including two timely 3-pointers, the kind of outside threat the Spurs were missing in Game 3. Johnson, the irrepressible 5-foot-11 point guard, had 14 points and 10 assists.

"We needed to get somebody on the perimeter to play well with all the attention Tim and David are going to get," Spurs coach Gregg Popovich said.

Led by Robinson, who showed he might not be as soft as some people believe, the Spurs won the rebounding race for the first time in the series, 49-34. The Spurs had 14 offensive rebounds.

Latrell Sprewell scored 26 points, and Marcus Camby had 20 points and 13 rebounds for the Knicks, who face elimination Friday night at the Garden.

"Offense was not the problem," Van Gundy said. "We got crushed on the boards."

Crushing the Knicks, finishing off this ragtag bunch that Larry Johnson referred to as "rebellious slaves," has been the most difficult task of these playoffs.

"We didn't want to give them any opportunity for life," Robinson said. "We came in concentrated and focused. It's a one-game thing, and we want to knock them out."

MARIO ELIE REJECTS ALLAN HOUSTON'S SHOT IN GAME 4 OF THE FINALS.

REBOUNDS

For the first time in the Finals, the San Antonio Spurs won the battle of boards in Game 4. Tim Duncan pulled down 18 rebounds and David Robinson 17 as the Spurs finished with 49 total rebounds (14 of them offensive) to the Knicks' 34. Above left, Tim Duncan (21), Allan Houston (20), Jaren Jackson (2) and Chris Childs (1) watch a rebound come off the rim. Above right, David Robinson pulls down a rebound over teammate Mario Elie and the Knicks' Latrell Sprewell during Game 2.

SPURS FANS FILL THE BARS ALONG THE RIVERWALK IN SAN ANTONIO DURING GAME 5 OF THE NBA FINALS.

GAME 5

SPURS 78, KNICKS 77

BY KEN BERGER   JUNE 26, 1999

NEW YORK (AP)—David Robinson and Tim Duncan embraced when it was over, savoring the thrilling ride propelled by the old-school guy and the young man with little flash but plenty of talent.

And quite a future.

The Spurs are no longer soft, weak, overrated or unappreciated. They are NBA champions for the first time, a team whose talent—and yes, toughness—caught up with their composure in a thrilling finale to a season that once seemed as though it might never happen.

"I've been privileged to play with two of the great players in this league," said Mario Elie, who earned his third championship ring Friday night when the Spurs beat the New York Knicks 78-77. "David was an MVP, and Tim obviously was the MVP this year. You guys that didn't vote for him should be ashamed of yourselves."

Duncan, who finished second to Utah's Karl Malone in the MVP voting this season, was second to no one in the finals. He scored 31 points and was named MVP of the finals, winning his first NBA title in his second season.

"It's a blessing to do what we did this year, and there's no guarantees I'll ever be back," said Duncan, talented enough to win the title and just hayseed enough to record the postgame celebration with a mini-cam.

Robinson, the other part of the Twin Towers, should have been the one rolling tape. It took him 10 years to win his championship.

"That one big goal that I had, achieving that goal, has been met," said Robinson, whose best accomplishment this season was checking his ego at the door and staying out of Duncan's way.

The Knicks—those incomparable, no-quit Knicks—didn't get out of the way in Game 5 until Latrell Sprewell missed one last awkward shot after catching the ball too far under the basket. The most thrilling game of a series that suffered from post-Michael Jordan TV ratings came down to the last shot, the way so many of Jordan's games did.

"We fought hard," Sprewell said. "We didn't want them to win on our court, but they played well. They deserved it. They were the best team this year."

Sprewell scored an incendiary 35 points that included a vicious dunk that nearly brought the house down at Madison Square Garden. On the game's final play, Charlie Ward's inbounds pass found Sprewell too far under the basket. Sprewell missed, and the Spurs stormed the court with their wives, children and girlfriends to celebrate.

"It's a journey that goes to show that hard work and persistence truly pays off," said Robinson, criticized during his career for not being able to lead his team to a title.

Avery Johnson, the journeyman who heard too many times that he'd never be a success in the NBA, calmly hit a corner jumper that put the Spurs ahead 78-77 with 47 second left. He described the Spurs as "a tough—you heard me everybody—tough basketball team."

Duncan averaged 27.4 points and 14 rebounds and didn't have to be slick like Allen Iverson or strong like Shaquille O'Neal to get a championship ring.

"I don't think there are words to describe Tim Duncan," Spurs forward Sean Elliott said. "He's not flashy, he's not in your face, he doesn't have to intimidate people. He just goes out and plays the game with a lot of style, a lot of class."

With an efficient, unflappable run of success in these playoffs, the Spurs ran off a 15-2 record that tied the second-best playoff run in NBA history. And while many of them preferred to savor the moment rather than dream of more titles to come, Mario Elie didn't mind.

"I tell the guys, `Enjoy this feeling. I know you're going to want to do this again,'" said Elie.

In their third game of the series at the Garden, it became clear near the end what the Spurs had on their minds.

Elie, who looked as pumped as a prize fighter before the game, hit a big 3-pointer in front of Knicks fan Spike Lee and made like Reggie Miller—glaring at the orange-clad film maker and giving him some of that New York City mouth.

Jackson, who preferred to relax and listen to headphones before taking the floor, hit a deep 3-pointer a few minutes before that.

Duncan was simply unstoppable. He scored seven straight Spurs points late in the third to keep the Knicks from building on a 4-point lead, then scored San Antonio's first three baskets of the fourth. Finally, he ran interference while his little buddy, the 5-foot-11 Johnson, hit the shot that decided the game.

"The main thing is, you have to know you're going to shoot it," Johnson said. "Don't hesitate, shoot it, let it go."

And let the celebration begin.

REFEREE JOE CRAWFORD (CENTER) AND COACHES JEFF VAN GUNDY (LEFT) AND GREGG POPOVICH DISCUSS A PROBLEM WITH THE SHOT CLOCKS DURING THE THIRD QUARTER OF GAME 5.

TIM DUNCAN GRABS A REBOUND WHILE NEW YORK'S LARRY JOHNSON LOOKS ON.

SPURS PLAYERS, INCLUDING DAVID ROBINSON (50), TIM DUNCAN (21), AND SEAN ELLIOTT (32) CELEBRATE AFTER TIME EXPIRES IN THEIR TITLE-CLINCHING VICTORY.

DAVID ROBINSON SHOOTS OVER KURT THOMAS (LEFT) AND CHRIS DUDLEY DURING THE SPURS' 78-77 VICTORY.

SPURS FANS WELCOME CHAMPIONS HOME

BY JIM VERTUNO   JUNE 26, 1999

SAN ANTONIO (AP)—The San Antonio Spurs came home Saturday to share their NBA championship trophy with a city starved for a winner.

The Spurs won their first NBA title in the franchise's 26-year history, beating the New York Knicks in five games in the finals. San Antonio clinched the series with a 78-77 victory Friday night that touched off a downtown celebration for which fans had ached.

That the Spurs won the series in New York's Madison Square Garden instead of the Alamodome mattered little to the thousands who greeted the team's plane at San Antonio International Airport Saturday afternoon.

Nor did it matter that the championship capped a lockout-shortened season in which the league was often criticized for sloppy play.

"It's about showing that nice guys do finish first. Hopefully, this is the start of a dynasty. There's a lot of pride with this. It's as important as the Alamo," fan Frank Cassiano said. "Remember the Alamo! Remember the Spurs!"

City merchants agreed. Downtown stores were fully stocked with Spurs championship T-shirts, and congratulatory banners hung in shop windows.

The Spurs returned the appreciation with a full-page ad in the *San Antonio Express-News* thanking fans for their support.

Police measured some of that support at more than 12,000 fans strong when the team arrived Saturday.

The crowd alternated between chanting "Go, Spurs, Go!" and singing Queen's "We Are The Champions" as the plane taxied onto the runway and pulled up to the gate.

Guard Avery Johnson, who hit the winning shot, was the first to emerge from the plane holding the gold NBA Championship trophy over his head.

Center David Robinson was right behind, and carried the trophy to a makeshift stage and thrust it over his head before passing it down so that fans could touch it.

"It's good to be home. You deserve this championship, San Antonio, you deserve this!" Robinson exclaimed. "We worked so hard to get here. I waited 10 years, the city waited 26."

Johnson said he has yet to settle down from his championship-winning shot with 47 seconds left in the game.

"My heart is beating a thousand times a minute," he told the crowd, who greeted him with chants of "M-V-P! M-V-P!"

"This is for people who make $12,000 a year and have been Spurs fans forever. This is about everybody in San Antonio, it's not just about us," Johnson said.

Just as he had immediately after the game Friday, Tim Duncan recorded the celebration on a video camera. Guard Steve Kerr, who won three championships with the Chicago Bulls, said post-game celebrations are becoming old hat.

"This is getting old for me," Kerr joked. "Thank you. This is a thrill for me. I feel like it just landed in my lap."

The team made only a 15-minute appearance before leaving in three team buses.

About two hours before the team's arrival, 3,000 fans were already waiting to greet the team on the tarmac. The throng happily withstood a slight drizzle, cheering and mugging for TV cameras long before the Spurs touched down. Later, fire trucks sprayed the crowd with water to take a little edge off the 88-degree heat that was up near 100 on the heat index.

The postgame victory celebration lasted into the early hours Saturday as thousands of fans poured onto downtown streets. Unlike other cities where sports celebrations have turned violent, San Antonio police reported no major incidents.

In a decade of repeat champions—the Chicago Bulls and Houston Rockets won eight titles between them in the 1990s—talk of a repeat had already begun.

"We've talked about it already. ... We'll be back in it again," Johnson said.

"It (winning) shuts up the critics who said they were too soft and could not win the championship. We're going to do it again," fan Mike Moreno said.

The city's celebrations were scheduled to continue Sunday with a downtown parade and a pep rally at the Alamodome.

TIM DUNCAN AND AVERY JOHNSON HUG IN THE LOCKER ROOM AFTER WINNING THE SPURS' FIRST NBA TITLE.

DAVID ROBINSON (LEFT) HOISTS THE NBA CHAMPIONSHIP TROPHY AS TIM DUNCAN HOLDS HIS FINALS MVP TROPHY AT MADISON SQUARE GARDEN.

AVERY JOHNSON HOLDS UP THE CHAMPIONSHIP TROPHY AND DAVID
ROBINSON HUGS THE SPURS MASCOT AS THE WORLD CHAMPION SPURS
RETURN TO SAN ANTONIO.

SAN ANTONIO CELEBRATES NBA TITLE

BY KELLEY SHANNON   JUNE 28, 1999

SAN ANTONIO (AP)—Spurs fans didn't want the party to end.

All weekend the city cheered the first NBA championship won by its only major league sports team after 26 years of struggle.

The celebration peaked Sunday night with a Fiesta-style river parade attended by 230,000 people and a tribute afterward for the team at the Alamodome.

"It feels good. Everything came together this year perfectly," Spurs center David Robinson told ecstatic parade-goers. "Our team came together. The city came together."

Players, coaches, team executives and a few devoted fans rode decorated, motorized barges along the San Antonio River through downtown as spectators lined the River Walk to watch. It was reminiscent of the city's annual Fiesta celebration each spring.

Avery Johnson, the 5-foot-11 point guard who hit the winning jump shot against the New York Knicks on Friday to capture the title, was the star of the show at the dome.

Johnson introduced his fellow players, cracked jokes about their personalities, made fun of the fact that he was twice cut by the Spurs and led approximately 40,000 fans in chants and cheers.

"I just want to ask you a question," Johnson said to the dome crowd. "Did the Lakers win the championship?"

"No," the fans yelled.

"Did the Portland Trail Blazers win the championship?"

"No," screamed the fans.

"Did the Utah Jazz win the championship?"

The crowd responded with a huge "No," and Johnson added, "With the Utah Jazz, it's all right to say 'Hell, no!'"

"I just want to ask you a question. ... Did the San Antonio Spurs win the championship?" Johnson asked.

The fans went wild.

The Spurs came to San Antonio in 1973 as part of the American Basketball Association and merged into the NBA in 1976. San Antonio is the first old ABA team to win an NBA title.

This was the team's first trip to the NBA Finals.

"It's been so fantastic to see David Robinson and Avery Johnson get their due," said 11-year season-ticket holder Kevin Conroy, who rescheduled his cancer radiation treatments so he could attend the NBA Finals.

Entering the Alamodome to the song, "We Are the Champions," Spurs players hopped onto a stage where the basketball court normally is and waved to the crowd as team members showed off the Larry O'Brien title trophy.

Robinson, a 10-year veteran, thanked the Spurs players of the past.

"One of the reasons I came here was because y'all had a tradition. The name I knew was George Gervin," Robinson said.

Gervin, a Hall of Fame member who played for the Spurs in the 1970s and early 1980s, stepped onto the stage and held the championship trophy as the crowd gave him big applause.

Tim Duncan was still recording everything with the mini-cam he also turned on after the Spurs' victory in Madison Square Garden. He was joined by several other Spurs, who pointed their cameras at the crowd.

"M-V-P, M-V-P," the fans chanted when Duncan was introduced.

Spurs coach Gregg Popovich told the fans they were crucial in the team's playoff victories, especially in urging on the game-winning, tippy-toe 3-pointer Sean Elliott sunk to defeat Portland in Game 2 of the Western Conference finals on Memorial Day.

"Without your energy, Sean Elliott can't stand on his toes and he misses that shot," Popovich said.

"When he hit that shot, it made it possible for Avery Johnson to hit another shot," the coach said.

And everyone knew what came next.

SPURS FANS CHEER AS THEY GREET THEIR TEAM AT THE AIRPORT ON SATURDAY, JUNE 26.

SEAN ELLIOTT LETS FANS AND TEAMMATE MALIK ROSE (RIGHT) TOUCH THE NBA CHAMPIONSHIP TROPHY.